Ultimate FACTIVITY Collection

MARVEL
SPIDER-MAN

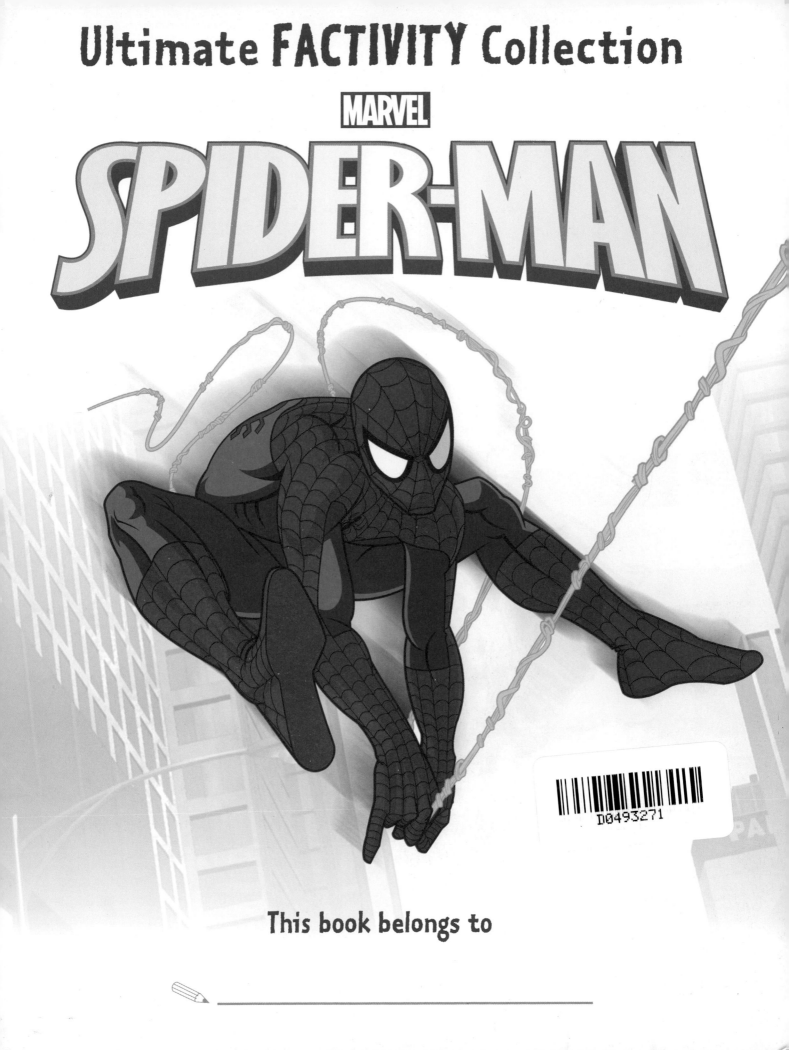

This book belongs to

_____

Spider-Man

Peter Parker was just a regular, geeky high school student until the day he was bitten by a radioactive spider. At that moment, he was transformed into a teenage Super Hero. He became... Spider-Man!

Peter Parker

Peter was a shy boy, with a big fear of heights. He loved to read comic books and dreamed of being like one of his favourite costumed heroes. But his whole world changed when he became Spider-Man!

Scientist Peter

Peter is a science genius – he even won a scholarship to Empire State University! He designs most of Spider-Man's crime-fighting gadgets himself.

The Daily Bugle

Sometimes even Super Heroes need an ordinary job! Peter sells his photographs of Spider-Man in action to *The Daily Bugle* newspaper.

Spider-Man's powers

When the spider bit Peter, it gave him all of its super powers. Suddenly Peter had incredible spider-like reflexes, strength and speed.

The costume

Do you recognise this famous costume? Peter designed his Spider-Man suit all by himself to match his spider-like powers.

Photography

Peter has always been creative. He is a master photographer, and is really good at taking dramatic photos.

Friends and family

Peter's friends and family are very important to him. It's tough for Peter to balance his love for them with the duties of being a hero!

Fact Challenge

Spider-Man's Story

Draw your own comic strip

Peter Parker is just an ordinary teenager. But when he is bitten by a radioactive spider at a science exhibition, Peter changes into a web-slinging Super Hero with amazing powers.

Read the comic strip and draw in the empty boxes.

Use these pictures to help you with your drawings.

Peter Parker

Peter has dark hair and wears formal school clothes and glasses.

Radioactive spider

This spider swung into a science experiment and got hit by a blast of radiation.

Peter Parker lives a happy life with his Uncle Ben and Aunt May.

Peter's only problem is being bullied by Flash.

One day...

...everything changes. Peter visits a science exhibit and is bitten by a radioactive spider.

You could give your characters **speech bubbles**

 4

Start drawing **lightly** with a **pencil** before you use coloured pens or pencils!

Peter realises he can sense when bad things are about to happen...

...and he can stick to the sides of buildings!

Peter is now strong, too. He becomes a wrestler.

He designs a costume that fits his new spider-like skills.

Then, Peter's Uncle Ben is shot by a robber.

Peter decides to use his powers to fight crime.

The city is safe now that Spider-Man is around.

Helpful pictures

The costume
Spider-Man wears a dazzling red and blue costume.

New York City
Spider-Man is totally at home among the New York City skyscrapers.

Fighting crime
Spider-Man uses his webs to capture nasty criminals who break the law.

Could Peter be **rescuing** someone from a criminal?

Spider Powers
Choose the right super power

The radioactive spider that bit Peter gave him quicker reflexes, spider-like senses and the ability to stick to walls. Combined with Peter's genius-level intellect, these abilities make Spider-Man a powerful force for good.

Find the stickers for each situation. Then, match the powers to the situations they would be used in.

Reflexes

Peter's reflexes are 40 times faster than an average human, allowing him to easily dodge attacks.

Wall crawling

Peter can attach himself to any surface, allowing him to climb walls and hang from ceilings.

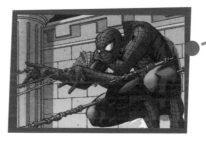

Web slinging

Peter designed his own web shooters so that he could swing from building to building.

Arachnid abilities

Peter's powers are enhanced spider abilities. Spiders are intelligent, and use webs and traps to catch their prey. They can also attach themselves to surfaces, move quickly and have very fast reflexes.

Spider-sense

When there is danger nearby, Spider-Man feels a strange tingling at the back of his head.

Draw lines through the centre of the web to link the powers to the situations.

Situation

Find the **stickers** at the back of the book.

Tall building

A hostage is being held on the top floor of a skyscraper. How will Spider-Man get to the top?

Invisible danger

There is a hidden threat approaching Spider-Man. What power would he use to detect it?

Fact Challenge

Emergency

Spider-Man needs to get to the scene of a crime, and fast! How would he travel there?

Battling an enemy

Spider-Man is battling against a villain. What power should he use to avoid their attacks?

Find the **answers** on page 97.

The Suit

Complete Spidey's suit

At first, the Spidey suit was just a simple stage costume that Peter designed – but now it's one of the coolest crime-fighting outfits around! This slick suit is a marvel of modern science, and a source of fear for evil-doers everywhere!

The mask

Spider-Man's mask hides his true identity. The eyepieces are made from one-way mirrors. This means Spider-Man's face can't be seen, but he can still see out.

You could colour in the **shading** around Spidey's muscles.

Complete Spider-Man's suit by colouring in the missing half.

Try to match the **red and blue** of the suit.

The belt

Spider-Man wears a belt hidden underneath his suit. It holds gadgets, including his spider-signal, spider-tracers and a miniature digital camera. It also has spare web fluid cartridges.

Gloves and boots

Spider-Man's gloves and boots are made of a thin layer of material, so that his hands and feet can still stick to walls through them. His web-shooters are hidden underneath his gloves.

Super Suits
Design a new suit for Spidey

Spider-Man has worn several different suits for his epic battles against evil. Each outfit gives him new abilities, which help him fight his many foes.

Read about Spider-Man's other suits to help you design your own.

Gloves conceal Spider-Man's **web-shooters**.

Armoured suit

This suit is covered in strong metal to protect the Super Hero from his enemies' weapons.

Stealth suit

Peter once developed a suit that could make him invisible. It helped him to sneak up on his enemies!

Iron Spider

Tony Stark (who also fights crime as the Super Hero Iron Man) made this suit for Spidey. It can deflect bullets, camouflage itself and even grows extra arms to help Spidey in battles!

Alien suit

This black suit is actually an alien life-form. It was able to react to Peter's thoughts and attach itself to his body when he needed it. The alien suit made Spidey's Super Hero skills even more powerful!

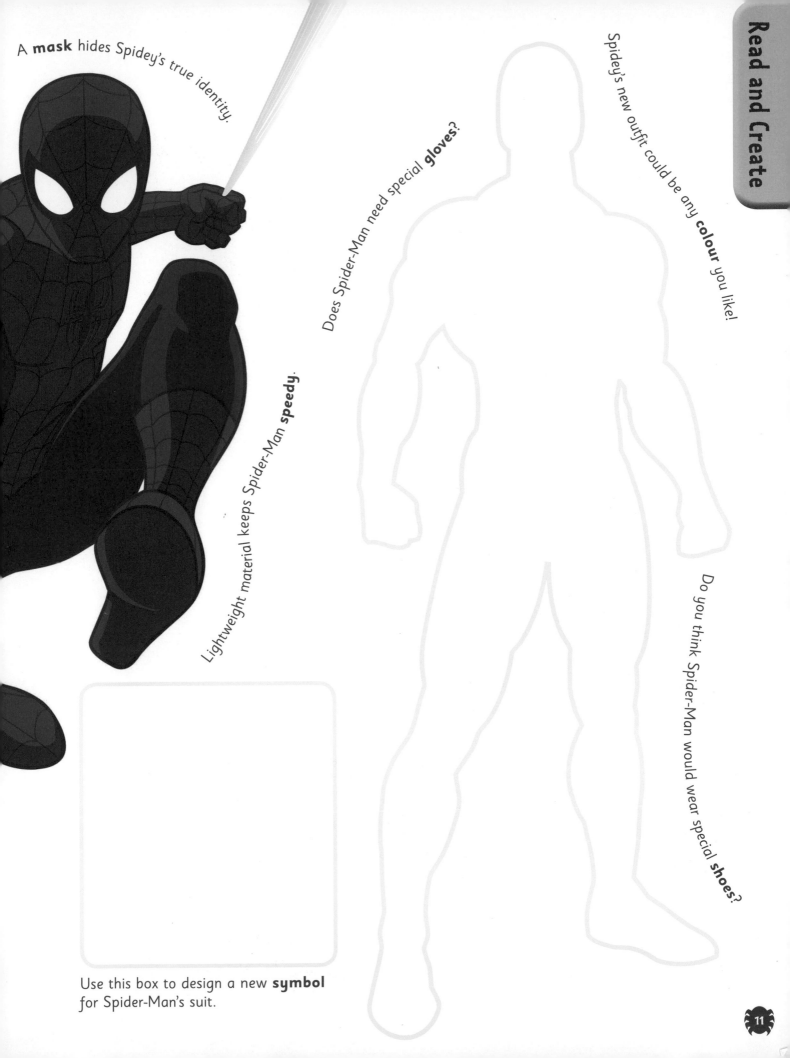

A **mask** hides Spidey's true identity.

Does Spider-Man need special **gloves**?

Spidey's new outfit could be any **colour** you like!

Lightweight material keeps Spider-Man **speedy**.

Do you think Spider-Man would wear special **shoes**?

Use this box to design a new **symbol** for Spider-Man's suit.

Master Photographer

Piece together Peter's photo

Peter Parker is an amazing photographer. He started selling his photographs to *The Daily Bugle* newspaper when he was still in high school. No one at the paper knows that Peter is really Spider-Man!

Taking photos for the Bugle is Peter's part-time job.

Web cam

Peter takes photos of Spidey's battles by placing his automatic camera in clever locations. He uses sticky spider webbing to fix the camera in place.

Peter's boss

The editor of *The Daily Bugle*, J. Jonah Jameson, hates Spider-Man. He writes newspaper stories that deliberately make Spider-Man look bad. Unfortunately for Peter Parker, J.J. Jameson is also his boss!

Action shots

As Spider-Man, Peter Parker is able to take incredible photos of other heroes and villains. As hard as they try, no one else in New York manages to get the photo opportunities he does!

J.J. has ripped up Peter's photo of Spider-Man battling a villain. Put it back together using stickers.

Spider-Man's spider-sense is **tingling**!

The villain has **sharp claws**, **red eyes** and a **very long tongue**.

The pair are crashing through a **brick wall**.

Find the **stickers** at the back of the book.

What animal is he fighting?

In this photo, Spider-Man is fighting a villain who looks like a type of animal. What is he?

Find the **answer** on page 97.

The Daily Bugle
Write your own newspaper story

Everyone in New York City reads *The Daily Bugle* newspaper. It often features exciting stories about Super Heroes and Villains. The editor-in-chief is grouchy J.J. Jameson.

J.J. thinks Spidey is dangerous and has accused him of many different crimes.

Read about a battle between Spider-Man and the Super Villain Electro, then write a newspaper story about it.

1 Lying in wait

- **Spider-Man** thinks **Electro** has **kidnapped** his Aunt May.
- He tracks down Electro at his **apartment**.
- The pair **fight** and Electro **blasts** the room apart!

2 Shocking attack

- The **battle** moves outside.
- Electro uses his **electricity** to **blow up** all of the cars on the **street**, creating a huge **fireball**.

3 Lights out

- Spider-Man **punches** Electro and stops his attacks.
- The innocent **people** on the street are **saved**, but a burning building **collapses** and **buries** Spidey and Electro!

4 Wounded warrior

- Spider-Man is **injured**.
- He is rushed to hospital in an **ambulance**, but Electro mysteriously **vanishes**.

You could try writing your story from **J.J.'s point of view**. It would say that Spider-Man is a **villain!**

DAILY BUGLE

New York City

MASKED MENACE
TERRORIZES NEW YORK CITY

SUPER VILLAIN ELECTRO DESTROYS CITY STREET

_____

_____

_____

_____

_____

_____

_____

_____

_____

_____

About The Editor:
J.J. Jameson

Editor-in-Chief
Concerned citizen
Loving father
Mayoral candidate
A name you can trust.

Spidey Challenge

Test your knowledge on this section

Answer each question. If you need help, look back through the section.

Now you have finished the first section of the book, take the Spidey Challenge to see if you are a true Spidey expert!

1 Find the sticker that best matches the description:

This suit that Spider-Man wore was actually an alien life-form.

2 Which of these is one of Spidey's powers?

Flying ☐   **Turning invisible** ☐   **Sticking to walls** ☐

3 The editor of *The Daily Bugle* is A.J. Jameson.

True ☐   **False** ☐

4 The eyepieces of Spider-Man's costume are made of

✏ _____

5 Name this character:

✏ _____

Find the **answers** on page 97.

Test your Knowledge

Use your stickers to create
your own Spider-Man scene!

Spidey in Action

Peter Parker has amazing spider-like powers that most people could only dream of having. As Spider-Man, he is one of the greatest Super Heroes around, so the criminals of New York City had better watch out!

Wall crawling

Spider-Man can crawl along any surface, no matter how smooth. This comes in particularly handy when sneaking up on a enemy!

Swinging into action

Spider-Man designed his own webbing and web shooters. He uses this incredibly strong material to swing through the city and capture bad guys.

Super strength

Spider-Man's amazing strength makes him a worthy opponent for any criminal. He can lift heavy objects and easily leap the height of three stories!

To the rescue!

Spider-Man's actions have saved countless lives. He thinks nothing of putting himself in terrible danger if innocent people are in trouble.

Find the **stickers** at the back of the book.

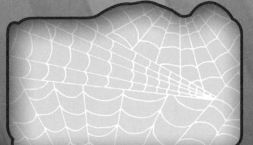

Speedy Spidey

Spider-Man can get to the scene of a crime faster than the fastest police car. He uses his webs to swing from building to building.

Fighting crime

Spider-Man has made it his mission to battle criminals wherever he finds them. There always seems to be a Super Villain for Spidey to defeat.

Sensing danger

When Spidey gets a strange tingling sensation in the back of his head, he knows danger is coming. He can use it to dodge an attack or detect trouble in the city.

Fact Challenge

Web Slinging
Draw Spider-Man's webs

Spider-Man uses his webbing in many different ways, depending on the danger. His webs allow him to swing quickly across New York City, capture criminals and protect innocent people from harm.

Read about the types of webbing. Then, draw the best webs for each situation in the boxes opposite.

Spidey's webbing is **strong** and **long-lasting**.

Web swinging

Spider-Man uses web swinging more than anything else. He can travel very quickly by using the rope-like strands to swing from building to building.

Web walls

Spider-Man can create entire walls of webbing for when he needs to stop a bad guy. He also uses it to prevent vehicles from crashing out of control.

Webbing backpack

When he needs to, Spider-Man can make useful objects out of webbing, like a webbing backpack that he attaches to himself.

Pressure webs

By rapidly pressing the trigger on his web shooters, Spider-Man can fire small balls of webbing at enemies. This will temporarily blind or confuse them.

Grapple webbing

If Spidey needs to grab someone, he fires a thick piece of web to wrap around them. He uses this to capture villains or to pull people to safety.

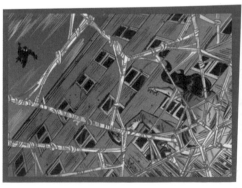

Web netting

Spider-Man can make large nets out of webbing, which he can use to save people who are falling from great heights.

Spider-Man wants to **confuse** Doctor Octopus. Draw the webbing he should shoot.

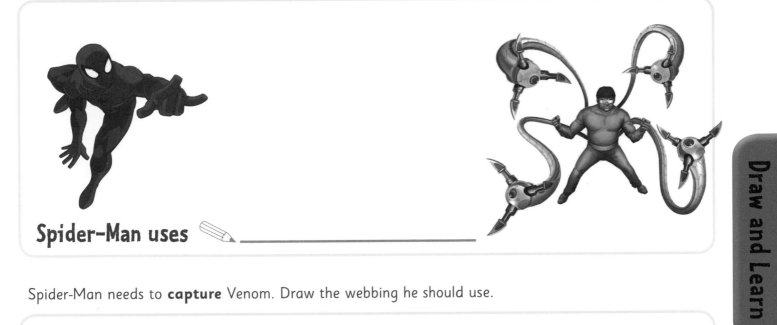

Spider-Man uses _____

Spider-Man needs to **capture** Venom. Draw the webbing he should use.

Spider-Man uses _____

MJ is **falling** from a rooftop! Draw how Spider-Man uses his webs to **save her**.

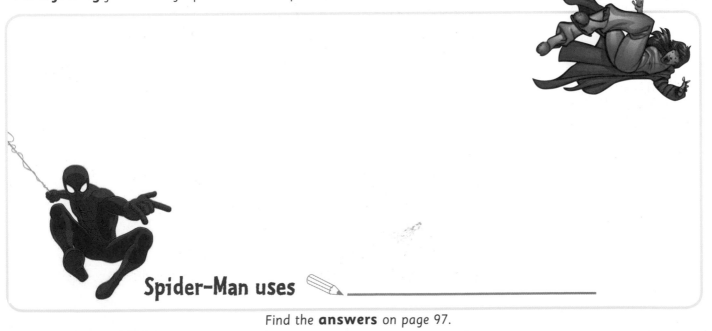

Spider-Man uses _____

Find the **answers** on page 97.

Rhino Rampage

Decide if the newspaper reporter's notes are true

The Rhino is one of Spidey's most powerful enemies. He has tough skin and is really strong, but he is not very smart. Stories of the destruction he causes often appear in *The Daily Bugle* newspaper.

Read the comic strip, then read the reporter's notes and write down if each one is true or false.

The Rhino escapes from the lab where he was created and goes on a rampage!

The police are powerless to stop him.

He swings in and grabs the Rhino by the horn...

Spider-Man watches the Rhino from a rooftop.

Rhino

The Rhino has super-tough skin that is also bulletproof. A team of scientists surgically attached it to his body to try and make him into the perfect assassin.

...And smashes him into the ground!

TONK!

But the Rhino breaks free from Spider-Man and charges off.

BOP!

The Rhino smashes cars out of his way. He manages to escape — for now...

Find the **answers** on page 97.

THE END!

REPORTER'S NOTES

1 THE RHINO AND SPIDER-MAN WERE WORKING TOGETHER TO COMMIT CRIMES.

_____

2 SPIDER-MAN GRABBED THE RHINO BY THE HORN ON HIS HEAD.

_____

3 SPIDER-MAN HELPED THE RHINO TO GET UP WHEN HE FELL OVER.

_____

4 THE POLICE COULD HAVE STOPPED THE RHINO IF SPIDER-MAN HADN'T GOT IN THE WAY.

_____

5 THE RHINO DESTROYED CARS THAT WERE PARKED ON THE STREET.

_____

6 THE RHINO MANAGED TO GET AWAY.

_____

Fact Challenge

23

Spider-Man vs Electro

Draw a Wanted poster

No matter how many times Spider-Man captures a Super Villain, somehow they always manage to escape from prison! The citizens of New York City must help Spider-Man track Electro down, but they need to be careful – Electro is a very dangerous criminal.

Read about Electro below, then use the information to complete the Wanted poster.

Electro wears a **green** and **yellow** suit.

Electro's mask is shaped like **bolts of lightning**.

Electro's powers

Ever since he was struck by lightning while working on a power line, Electro has had the ability to control electricity. He can even shoot bolts of lightning from his fingertips to injure his foes.

Defeating Electro

Spider-Man has discovered ways to protect himself from Electro's lightning attacks. This includes battling the villain in the air, as electricity can only shock things that are touching the ground, or wearing rubber gloves to block electricity!

Draw **Electro** on the poster below.

WANTED: ELECTRO

Draw Electro's **mask** and **costume**.

The Super Villain Electro has escaped from prison! He is wearing a

✏ _____ suit and a ✏ _____ shaped

like lightning bolts. He should be considered extremely dangerous.

He has the ability to ✏ _____. If seen, do

not approach him, unless you are wearing ✏ _____ .

REWARD: $10,000,000

Find the **answers** on page 97.

Spider-Sense
Help Spidey cross the city

In New York City, trouble can be lurking around any corner. When Peter Parker needs to make his way to work as a scientist at Horizon Labs, he often runs into situations that only his spider-sense can deal with!

Read the instructions to begin the mission.

The mission

1. Grab something to use as a counter, and place it at the start.

2. Ask a friend to join you on your mission and decide who will go first.

3. Take turns to roll a die, then move the number of spaces that are shown on the die.

4. Be the first person to reach Horizon Labs.

5. Watch out for hazards along the way!

Start

1

2

Mary Jane gives you a kiss and puts a spring in your step. Move forward 2 spaces.

3

You sense a little old lady is about to be robbed. You stop to help her. Miss a go.

4

5

6

There's a road block ahead. You must swing over it. Leap forward a space.

7

8

You sense someone is in trouble, then discover it's Green Goblin laying a trap. Go back 3 spaces.

9

10

A crazy Spidey fan starts chasing you and you have to swoop away. Move forward 2 spaces.

11

12

13

14

15

16

Strange feeling

Spider-Man gets a tingling feeling at the back of his head that warns him of danger. This can alert him to situations almost before they happen.

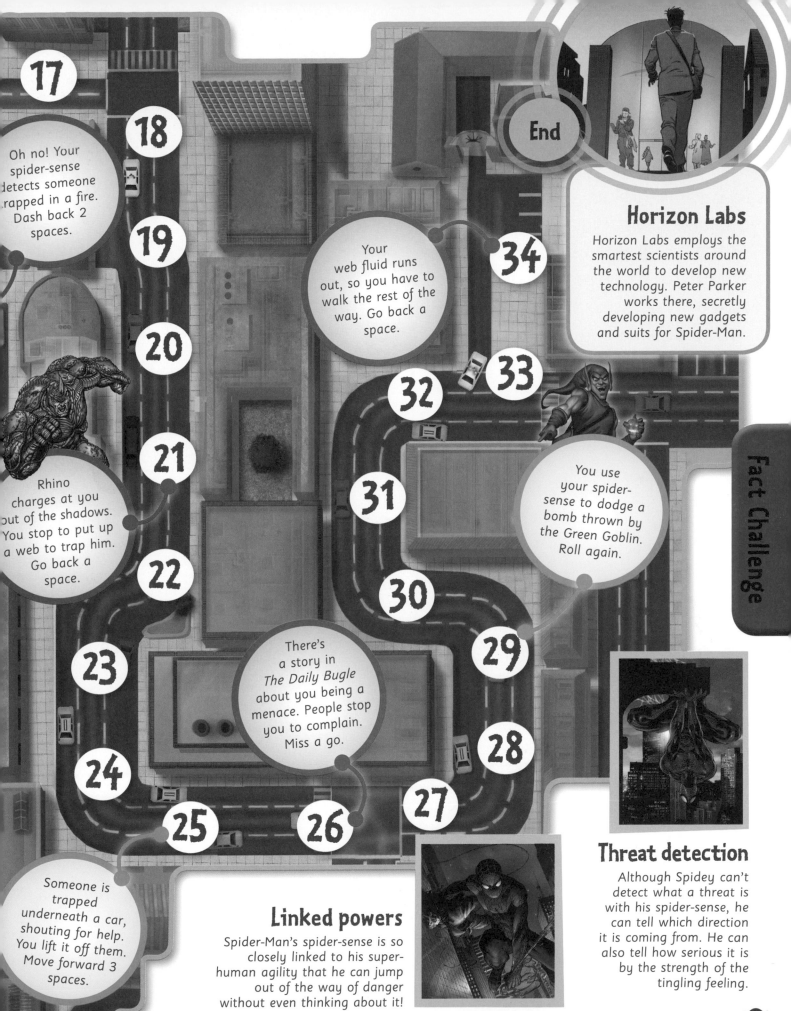

17

18

Oh no! Your spider-sense detects someone trapped in a fire. Dash back 2 spaces.

19

20

21

Rhino charges at you out of the shadows. You stop to put up a web to trap him. Go back a space.

22

23

24

25

26

Someone is trapped underneath a car, shouting for help. You lift it off them. Move forward 3 spaces.

Your web fluid runs out, so you have to walk the rest of the way. Go back a space.

34

33

32

31

30

29

28

27

There's a story in *The Daily Bugle* about you being a menace. People stop you to complain. Miss a go.

You use your spider-sense to dodge a bomb thrown by the Green Goblin. Roll again.

End

Horizon Labs

Horizon Labs employs the smartest scientists around the world to develop new technology. Peter Parker works there, secretly developing new gadgets and suits for Spider-Man.

Fact Challenge

Linked powers

Spider-Man's spider-sense is so closely linked to his super-human agility that he can jump out of the way of danger without even thinking about it!

Threat detection

Although Spidey can't detect what a threat is with his spider-sense, he can tell which direction it is coming from. He can also tell how serious it is by the strength of the tingling feeling.

Venom Face-Off

Finish the comic strip

Venom is an evil alien life-form. He looks like a black gooey liquid until he bonds with humans. He takes people over and enhances their abilities. He particularly hates Spider-Man, and loves unleashing terror on the streets of New York.

Venom is an evil creature.

Read the story, then write and draw the ending.

Use these images to help you.

Alien being

Venom is an alien symbiote. He takes over humans' bodies and uses them as a host.

Eddie Brock

Venom's main host is Eddie Brock. Eddie is a reporter who hates Spider-Man.

Draw lightly with a **pencil** before you use coloured pens or pencils.

Spider-Man knows that Venom will come after him, so he waits patiently.

Hello Spider-Man. I've been looking forward to this for a long time!

Venom mocks Spider-Man, and threatens his friends and family.

Once I'm finished with you, I'll go and visit Aunt May and MJ...

Eddie Brock reveals himself, and taunts Spider-Man.

Spider-Man manages to knock Venom off balance...

I'm still in here, and I haven't forgotten what you did to me!

...But Venom is stronger and faster than Spidey.

How will the story **end**? You **decide!**

THE END!

Terrifying creature
Venom is a horrifying monster. He has a huge mouth full of razor-sharp white teeth.

Venom webbing
Venom once used Spidey as a host. Venom is still able to shoot webbing like Spider-Man.

Venom symbol
Venom's signature look is a black suit with a white spider symbol – something he took from the time Spidey was his host.

Other symbiotes
Venom made other symbiotes, which took the names Toxin and Carnage.

Wall Crawler

Find the stickers of the villains and Spidey

Spider-Man is an expert climber, and can scale almost anything — even skyscrapers full of villains and other obstacles!

Spider-Man has made it to the top! But he can't stop to catch his breath — first he must beat the insane Green Goblin.

The Lizard hates all humans, and can whip his tail at 70 miles (110km) per hour! This savage villain will take all of Spider-Man's strength to beat.

The Scorpion is super-strong, but against a Super Hero who can stick to anything, he doesn't stand much of a chance.

For anyone else, a fire would be a massive obstacle, but not for wall-crawling Spidey. He can leap right over it.

How does Spider-Man defeat a crazy villain with four robotic arms? He can climb up and then drop on Doctor Octopus from above.

Kraven might be a mighty hunter, but Spider-Man can dodge his bullets, and then kick him out of the window.

Super sticky

Spidey is able to stick to any surface, helping him to crawl up buildings. When Spidey is stuck to something, it is nearly impossible to remove him.

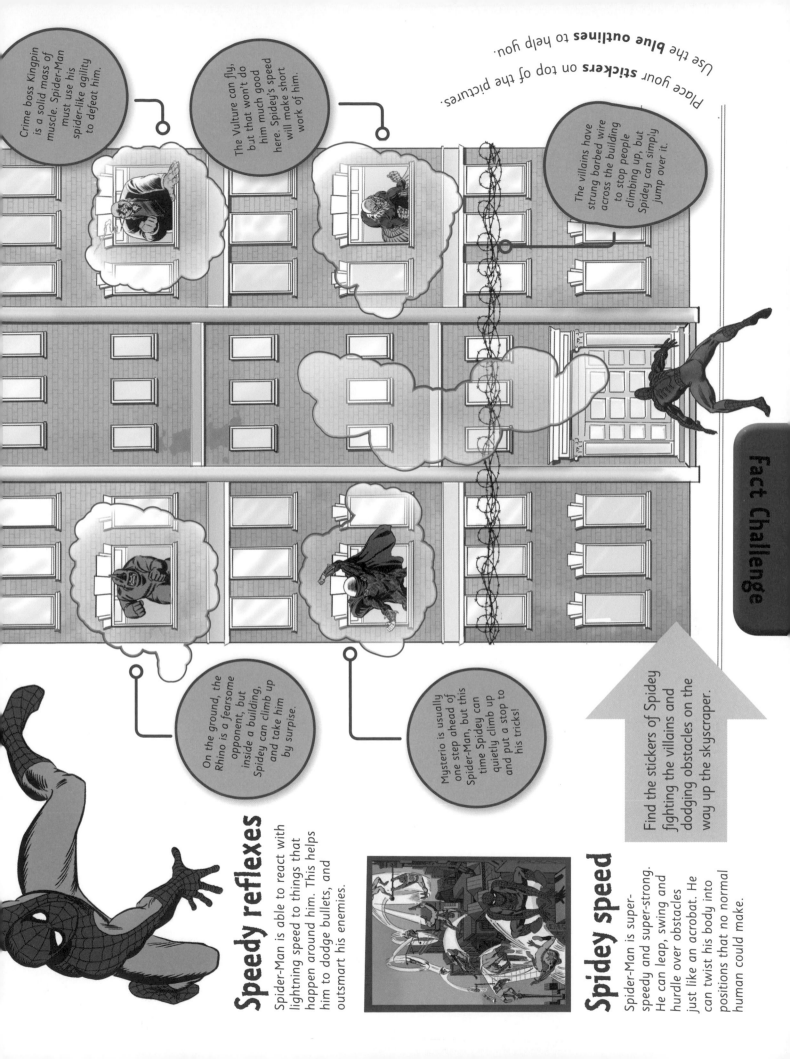

Spidey Challenge

Test your knowledge on this section

Answer each question. If you need help, look back through the section.

Now you have finished the second section of the book, take the Spidey Challenge to see how much you know about Spidey!

 **1** Find the sticker that best matches the description:

This villain's skin is so tough that it is bulletproof.

 2 Electro shoots bolts of lightning from his...

Eyes ⬜ **Fingertips** ⬜ **Mouth** ⬜

3 Venom has a spider web symbol on his chest.

True ⬜ **False** ⬜

 **4** Spidey gets a tingling feeling at the back of his

 _____ when he senses danger.

 **5** Name this type of webbing:

_____

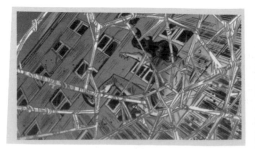

Find the **answers** on page 97.

Test your Knowledge

Use your stickers to create your own Spider-Man scene!

Spidey and Friends

It's a tough job being a Super Hero. Whether it's as Spider-Man, or as Peter Parker, Spidey needs people to turn to in tricky times. He calls on friends, family and sometimes even other Super Heroes.

May and Ben Parker

When Peter's parents died, Aunt May raised Peter with Uncle Ben. Now Uncle Ben has passed away, Peter is protective of Aunt May.

The Black Cat

Black Cat was once Peter's girlfriend. She has saved Spider-Man many times and been his friend when no one else trusted him.

Future Foundation

This Super Hero team got their powers from cosmic rays. As well as Spidey, the group includes Mister Fantastic, the Invisible Woman, the Human Torch and the Thing.

The Avengers

Spider-Man is also a member of another team of Super Heroes – the Avengers. Its members include Iron Man, Captain America, Hawkeye, Wolverine and Thor. They help Spidey if he is in trouble.

Daredevil

Spider-Man and Daredevil have fought together against enemies such as Kingpin and Electro. Daredevil is blind, but his other senses are super-powerful.

Mary Jane Watson

MJ is Peter's girlfriend. She is often a target for Spidey's foes because they know he loves her more than anything else.

Harry Osborn

Harry is Peter's best friend. They went to the same university, where they were roommates. Harry's father is secretly a Super Villain called The Green Goblin.

Fact Challenge

Rescue Mary Jane
Write the speech bubbles

Mary Jane is Peter Parker's best friend and girlfriend. Many of Spider-Man's enemies have tried to harm MJ to get to Spider-Man.

Mary Jane

MJ is a successful fashion model. She understands Peter better than anyone, and is one of the few people who knows that he is really Spider-Man.

You could **write** in pencil first and then use a pen.

The Green Goblin has kidnapped MJ!

Decide what each character will say and write it in the blank speech bubbles.

He is threatening to throw her off a bridge!

I've found the perfect bridge to throw Mary Jane off. Do you think you'll miss her, Spider-Man?

Spider-Man pleads with the Green Goblin to stop his crazy plans.

But the Green Goblin won't listen. Spidey shoots his webbing at the Green Goblin's Glider and brings him crashing to the ground.

Spider-Man and the Green Goblin fight. Spidey must save MJ, but the Green Goblin will do all it takes to conquer Spidey.

Spider-Man defeats the Green Goblin! MJ is safe! She thanks Peter for saving her life.

THE END!

Heroic Allies
Spot the heroes

Spider-Man has many amazing friends, including some who have incredible super powers of their own. These heroes sometimes join forces with Spidey to battle against evil together.

Read about Spidey's allies. Then use the clues to identify each hero.

Daredevil

This acrobatic Super Hero was blinded as a child. His senses of hearing, touch and smell became super-powerful to compensate. Heroic Daredevil feels no fear!

Spider-Girl

Spider-Girl got her powers from a sorcerer of a mysterious spider cult. She is strong and speedy, has spider-sense, and she can shoot webbing, too.

Scarlet Spider

This clone of Spider-Man has become a Super Hero himself. He has exactly the same powers as Spidey — he is super-fast, strong and he can climb walls.

The Black Cat

The Black Cat used to be a cat burglar, but now she's a hero (most of the time). The Black Cat has the ability to make bad luck strike her foes.

I am very strong.

I can climb up walls.

I am a clone.

Find my **sticker** at the back of the book.

?

1 My name is:

_____

38

I have the colour red on my costume.

I am acrobatic.

I am fearless.

I have long hair.

My costume is black and white.

I used to be a burglar.

I have the powers of a spider.

I can shoot webbing.

I wear a black mask.

2 My name is:

_____

3 My name is:

_____

4 My name is:

_____

Find the **answers** on page 97.

A New Partner

Design a new Super Hero

Over the years, Spider-Man has partnered with many different Super Heroes with all types of super powers. Like Spidey, their costumes are designed to show off their powers, and to make them look strong and heroic.

Read about some other Super Heroes, then draw a new Super Hero to battle alongside Spidey.

Iron Man

Iron Man built his costume of powered **armour**. It makes him **super-strong** and able to **fly**. He can also fire **lasers** from his hands.

The Thing

The Thing's orange skin looks like lots of **rocks**. Almost nothing can get through The Thing's **tough shell** – including bullets!

The Wasp

The Wasp can **shrink** to a tiny size or **expand** to a gigantic height. Her costume is in the colours of a wasp, and she can even grow **wings**.

The Human Torch

The Human Torch's costume is bright red and bursting with **flames** that can protect him. The Torch has the power to control **fire**.

Spider-Man's new partner is called:

A **mask** or **disguise** will hide their identity.

Write down what **powers** your Super Hero has. How about super-strength, the ability to fly or the power to see into the future?

You could include **gadgets** such as a jet pack!

Horizon Labs
Invent something for Spidey

Peter works at Horizon Labs, a company that creates advanced technology. His friends who work there are brilliant inventors. Peter uses Horizon Labs to design new gadgets and suits for Spider-Man.

Read about some of Peter Parker's inventions, then invent something of your own.

Peter's colleagues
The owner of Horizon Labs is the scientific genius Max Modell. The other talented employees work alongside Peter, but don't know that he is really Spider-Man.

Stealth suit
This suit can bend light and sound, making Spidey invisible and silent. The green lights allow him to be seen by allies if they wear special lenses.

Unstable molecule suit
Spider-Man made this suit so that he could wear it as a normal item of clothing. It changes colour when he wants to become Spider-Man.

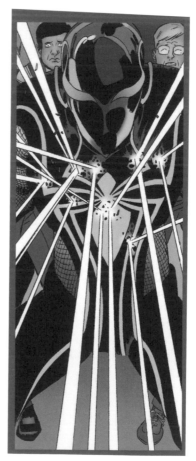

Spider-Armour Mk II
Peter used this armour when he temporarily lost his spider-sense. It is bulletproof, and has built-in web shooters.

Spider-Armour Mk III
This armour is insulated against electricity. It has jet boosters in the feet to allow Spidey to fly, and a holographic visor.

Thermoreactive foam balls

This weapon releases a special foam which turns hot things cold, and cold things hot.

Spider-Glider

Peter based the Spider-Glider on the glider used by the Green Goblin. It is a flying platform in the shape of a spider.

Left shooter — net!

Right — web barrage!

Voice-activated web shooters

Spider-Man designed web shooters with a voice-activation function so he could fire them just by speaking.

Cryo shooter

Peter developed the Cryo shooter to defeat the Super Villain Hydro-Man. It can freeze anything it hits almost instantly.

Why don't you invent something to help Spidey **fight** crime?

You could design some kind of **vehicle** for Spidey.

How about something to **capture** villains?

My new invention is:

The Avengers
Colour in Spidey's teammates

A great hero knows when it will take more than just his own powers to defeat an enemy. Spider-Man has often fought as part of Super Hero teams to defeat major threats. He is a member of the mightiest team of all – the Avengers.

Read about Spidey's Avengers teammates. Next, find them in the battle scene and colour them in.

1 Spider-Woman
There's not one but two spider-like heroes in this super team! Unlike Spidey, Spider-Woman has wings that help her to glide into action.

2 Iron Man
Spidey's ally wears a powerful suit of red and gold armour. He doesn't always get along with the other Avengers, but he is a vital member.

3 Wolverine
This mutant Super Hero has razor-sharp claws and animal instincts. He likes to think of himself as a lone wolf, but he and Spider-Man make a great team.

4 Thor
The God of Thunder often stands alongside Spider-Man in the Avengers. He has awesome physical powers, and wields an enchanted hammer.

5 Captain America
Spider-Man has long admired this noble red, white and blue hero. The web-slinger can even get a little starstruck when he partners with Cap.

6 Hawkeye
Hawkeye is a master archer. He can fire multiple arrows at a target with incredible accuracy. He is also a skilled martial artist and acrobat.

Super Base

Design a new base for Spidey

A Super Hero team needs somewhere safe to train and prepare for missions. Spidey and his Avengers teammates had their high-tech headquarters in this grand mansion – until it was destroyed by a crazed villain!

Read about the Avengers Mansion. Then design a new base for the team.

Living quarters

Screening devices monitor all visitors to the mansion. Inside, there are bedrooms for the Avengers and the butler's quarters, too.

Hangar

The top floor has a take-off and landing dock for the Avengers' Quinjets.

The gym

The building boasts a fully equipped gym with Olympic-sized swimming pool.

Operating theatre

Expert medical care and equipment is always on hand if the heroes are injured in battle.

Battle training

The team practise fighting techniques in this extra-protected room.

Assembly room

The Avengers' secret meetings are held here. They install the latest security devices to make sure the room is totally private.

Secure room

Members can hide here if any foes break into the mansion. It is almost impossible to get into!

Arsenal chamber

The heroes store and test their weapons and armour on the lowest floor. Next door, Hawkeye practises his archery in the firing range.

Spider-Man's new team base is called

Your new base will need to be **secure** and **well-defended**. The team members will need somewhere to **train**.

Perhaps you could give them a **hangar** to store their **vehicles**?

The team should also have some rooms to **live in**.

Spidey Challenge
Test your knowledge on this section

Answer each question. If you need help, look back through the section.

Now you have finished the third section of the book, take the Spidey Challenge to prove your Spider-Man knowledge.

1 Find the sticker that best matches the description:

This member of the Avengers has razor sharp claws.

2 Peter's girlfriend, Mary Jane, is a...

Teacher ☐   **Fashion model** ☐   **Photographer** ☐

3 Horizon Labs creates advanced technology.

True ☐   **False** ☐

4 The Human Torch has the power to control

✏ _____

5 Name this Super Hero:

✏ _____

48

Find the **answers** on page 97.

Use your stickers to create your own Spider-Man scene!

Test your Knowledge

Spider-Man's Foes

Spider-Man defends New York City from a huge number of enemies and evil-doers, many of whom are as unusual and powerful as Spider-Man himself. They will do whatever it takes to beat Spider-Man!

The Green Goblin

The Green Goblin is completely insane and obsessed with Spider-Man. He is possibly Peter Parker's greatest and most dangerous foe.

Doctor Octopus

Doctor Octopus is a scientific genius with four immensely strong mechanical arms.

The Sinister Six

The Sinister Six is a group created by Doctor Octopus. He gathered together five other Super Villains who had all been defeated by Spider-Man.

Sandman

The Sandman's body has been turned into radioactive sand, so he can transform into any size or shape.

Find the **stickers** at the back of the book.

The Vulture

The Vulture wears a homemade electromagnetic harness that allows him to fly, and also gives him enhanced strength and endurance.

Mysterio

Mysterio is possibly the weirdest of Peter's enemies. He relies on special effects and an arsenal of bizarre weaponry to battle Spider-Man.

The Scorpion

The Scorpion wears a battle suit that gives him super strength. The suit also gives him lightning-quick reflexes, and shields him from bullets.

The Chameleon

The Chameleon is a master of disguise. He uses realistic face masks or holograms to take on the appearances of his different victims.

The Green Goblin

Design a new Goblin-Glider

The Green Goblin is probably Spider-Man's most dangerous enemy. He is obsessed with defeating Spidey! He invents lots of gadgets to battle the web-slinger, including a speedy Goblin-Glider.

Look at the Green Goblin's Glider, then design a new one.

Magnetic clasps keep the Goblin's feet in place.

*Green Goblin's hands are free to throw **bombs**.*

*Spiky wings make the Glider look like a scary **bat**.*

Unmasked

The Green Goblin is scientist Norman Osborn in disguise. He got covered in a chemical that makes him very strong and clever, but also drove him mad. He uses his powers for evil.

The Glider

The Goblin-Glider travels very fast and helps the Green Goblin keep up with super-speedy Spidey. It comes complete with razor-sharp wings, which make for terrifying aerial attacks.

Glider in action

The Glider is activated by voice controls. It carries hidden weapons, like heat-seeking missiles that the Green Goblin can fire at his enemies.

Goblin's weapons

The Green Goblin's most famous weapons are pumpkin bombs, which look like Jack-O'-Lanterns. He carries them and other weapons in his "bag of tricks".

*Use this outline to **design** a new **Goblin-Glider**.*

*Will your Glider be based on an **animal**?*

*Add some **weapons** like spikes, bombs or missiles!*

Caught on Camera
Identify the Super Villains

Peter Parker relies on the pictures he takes of New York's Super Villains for his job at *The Daily Bugle*. His photographs show these criminals in all of their bizarre and terrifying glory.

Identify the villain in each zoomed-in picture.

Read about the villains and find their stickers at the back of the book.

Spidey's enemies are powerful and dangerous!

Kingpin

This **bald** crime boss may not have any super powers, but he makes up for it with his massive size and great strength. He dresses to impress in **fur**.

Mysterio

Mysterio uses tricks and gadgets to confuse and attack his enemies. His **helmet** is made of glass that allows him to see out but stops others seeing in.

The Scorpion

The Scorpion wears a **green battle suit** that gives him super strength. It has a powerful **tail** that he uses as a deadly weapon.

Kraven

This expert hunter wears the **skins** of his latest **prey**. He drinks potions that make him very strong. He won't stop until he defeats Spidey.

Carnage

This horrifying **red** monster is a lethal combination of an alien life-form and a killer named Cletus Kasady. He has **razor-sharp nails** and **pointed teeth**.

The Vulture

The Vulture's **bird costume** may look funny, but he is a serious inventor. He uses his **winged harness** to commit daring robberies.

1 Feathered foe

2 Meet the boss

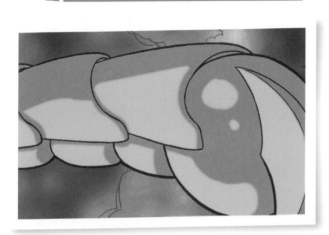

3 Stinging sensation

4 Master of illusion

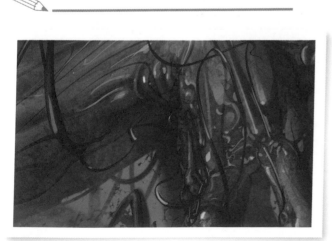

5 Bloody butcher

6 A skilled huntsman

Find the **answers** on page 97.

Sandman

Complete Sandman's arms

Sandman got his powers in a nuclear accident, and found that his whole body had been turned into sand! He can transform his body into any shape, including all kinds of scary weapons.

Shape-shifting

Sandman often turns his forearms into weapons like giant hammers, fists and clubs. He can also absorb nearby sand to make himself bigger, and change his density from hard to soft in an instant.

Draw Sandman's arms as weapons to complete the pictures.

You could draw **sand** blasting at enemies.

How about drawing something **spiky**?

What **other shapes** could he make?

Make Sandman's **arms** any length you like.

57

Secret Identities
Spot the Super Villain

It isn't just Super Heroes who have secret identities – Super Villains do, too. You can often see the reason why someone became a villain by looking at their secret identity. Many of them were not always evil!

Work out which Super Villain identity belongs to each person. Find the stickers at the back of the book.

Curt Connors

Curt Connors was a gifted army surgeon before he lost an arm in an accident. Afterward, Curt focused his energy on experiments to re-grow human limbs as **reptiles** are able to.

Norman Osborn

As a child, Osborn suffered from nightmares about a giant **goblin-like** monster. He is now a wealthy businessman and scientist, but he only cares about getting revenge on Spider-Man.

Slimy and green, this villain isn't pretty.

*This villain rides a **Glider** to chase Spidey.*

1 I am _____

2 I am _____

Super Villains

Electro
This Super Villain attacks his enemies with blasts of electricity, but he still feels inferior to Spider-Man.

The Green Goblin
The Green Goblin used his childhood memories to design a goblin mask to terrify people.

Venom
Venom is a horrifying combination of an alien life-form, and a man filled with hate.

The Lizard
Despite his ferocious appearance, Lizard was once a normal human, and a skilled doctor.

Max Dillon
Max once dreamed of becoming an **electrical** engineer, but his mother told him he wasn't smart enough. Max really wants respect and glory, but rarely gets either.

Eddie Brock
Eddie Brock was a reporter before Spidey revealed his stories were made up. Eddie hates Spider-Man, so he is the perfect host for a strange **alien creature** who also hates Spidey.

Fact Challenge

This villain's costume is the same **colour** as his work overalls.

Someone with a **long tongue** goes here.

3 I am ✎ _____

4 I am ✎ _____

Find the **answers** on page 97. **59**

Doctor Octopus
Draw Doctor Octopus's arms

Otto Octavius was a respected scientist. He built a set of four robotic arms so that he could do dangerous experiments at a distance, but a lab accident attached them to his body and turned him into a villain! He now uses his arms for evil – to battle Spidey and commit crimes.

Draw Doctor Octopus's other three robotic arms, and add stickers of things for them to grab!

Mental control
Doctor Octopus controls his mechanical arms simply by using the power of his mind.

Evil genius
Otto designed his arms himself. He is the most intelligent of all Spider-Man's enemies.

Armed and dangerous
Doctor Octopus's extra arms give him a big advantage in his battles against Spider-Man.

Doc Ock's arms are **super-strong**.

Doc Ock can pick up **large** or **small**, delicate things.

The arms are made of **shiny metal**.

A New Threat
Create a new Super Villain

Spidey has made countless enemies from his efforts to protect New York City. Dangerous new Super Villains are always emerging, with all kinds of destructive powers and mysterious intentions.

Learn about some of Spider-Man's foes, then design a new Super Villain to battle Spider-Man.

The Chameleon
The Chameleon can perfectly **copy anybody**. He can pretend to be other people using **masks** and disguises, and he copies their voices, too.

Hydro-Man
Hydro-Man has the ability to turn his body **into liquid** whenever he wants. He can attack people by **spraying** particles of his body at them under huge pressure.

Shocker
Shocker wears a special pair of **gauntlets** on his arms. They fire out powerful blasts of vibration to shock his enemies. His **suit protects** him by absorbing the shock.

The Lizard
The Lizard has razor-sharp **teeth** and **claws**. He can use his tail as a weapon to smash things. He can also **re-grow** limbs, and control the minds of other reptiles.

Spider-Man's new enemy is called:

✏️ _____

Write down what **powers** your Super Villain has. What about the ability to change shape, shoot flames or control people's minds?

_____

_____

_____

_____

Villains often carry **special equipment**, like swords.

Many Super Villains are based on **animals**.

63

Spidey Challenge
Test your knowledge on this section

Answer each question. If you need help, look back through the section.

Now you have finished the last section of the book, take the Spidey Challenge to show what you have learnt.

1 Find the sticker that best matches the description:

This villain transforms his arms into weapons to battle enemies.

2 How many robotic arms does Doctor Octopus have?

Four ⬜ **Six** ⬜ **Eight** ⬜

3 The Green Goblin is Neville Osborn in disguise.

True ⬜ **False** ⬜

4 The Lizard can control the _____ of other reptiles.

5 Which of Spidey's foes is this?

_____

Find the **answers** on page 97.

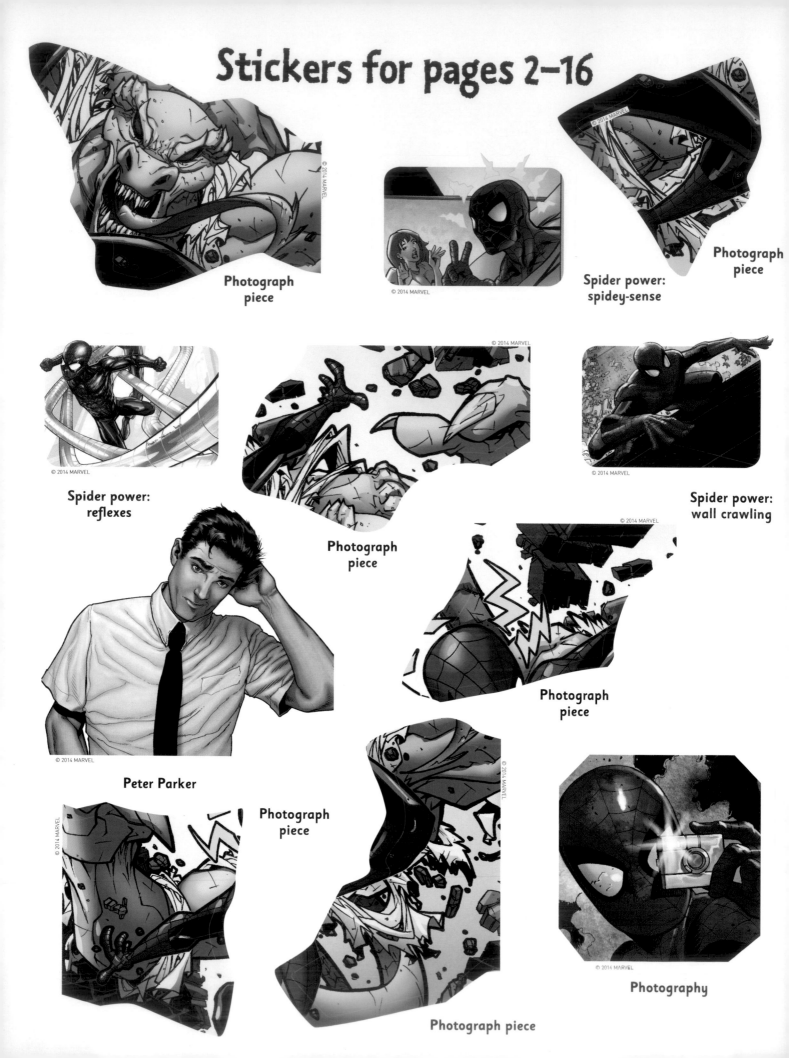

Stickers for pages 2–16

Photograph piece

Spider power: spidey-sense

Photograph piece

Spider power: reflexes

Photograph piece

Spider power: wall crawling

Peter Parker

Photograph piece

Photograph piece

Photograph piece

Photography

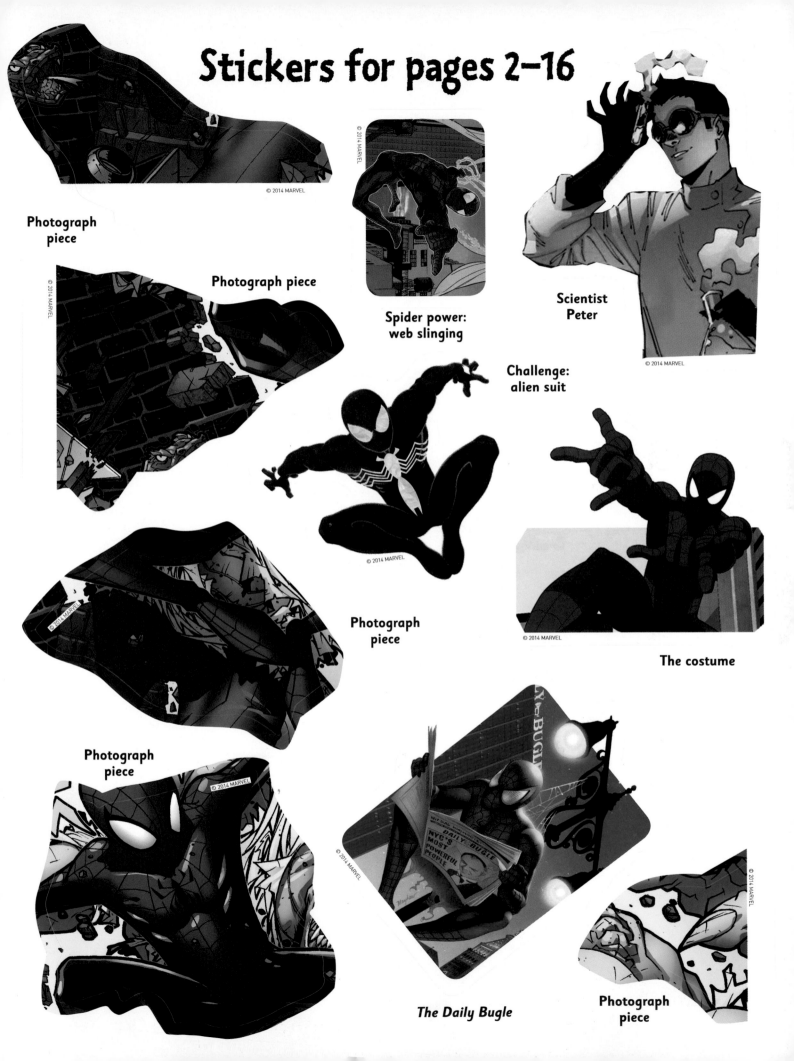

Stickers for pages 2–16

Photograph
piece

Photograph piece

Spider power:
web slinging

Scientist
Peter

Challenge:
alien suit

Photograph
piece

The costume

Photograph
piece

Photograph
piece

The Daily Bugle

Photograph
piece

Stickers for pages 2–16

Friends and family

Spider-Man's powers

Extra stickers

Stickers for pages 18–32

Wall crawler: flames

Wall crawling

Spidey and Kingpin

Spidey and the Scorpion

Spidey and the Vulture

Challenge: the Rhino

Spidey and Mysterio

To the rescue

Sensing danger

Spidey and Kraven

Spidey and Doctor Octopus

Speedy Spidey

Spidey and the Rhino

Spidey and the Green Goblin

CHOOM!

Super strength

Stickers for pages 18–32

**Wall crawler:
barbed wire**

**Fighting
crime**

**Spidey
and the
Lizard**

**Swinging
into action**

Extra Stickers

Extra stickers

Stickers for pages 34-48

Mary Jane Watson

Harry Osborn

Fearless hero

Cat burglar

Masked hero

The Avengers

Spidey's clone

Challenge: Wolverine

May and Ben Parker

Daredevil

Black Cat

Future Foundation

Extra stickers

Extra stickers

Stickers for pages 50-64

Slimy villain

Caught on Camera: Kraven

Mysterio

The Sinister Six

Challenge: Sandman

Caught on Camera: The Vulture

Engineer villain

The Vulture

The Chameleon

Caught on Camera: Carnage

Caught on Camera: The Scorpion

Scientist villain

Doctor Octopus

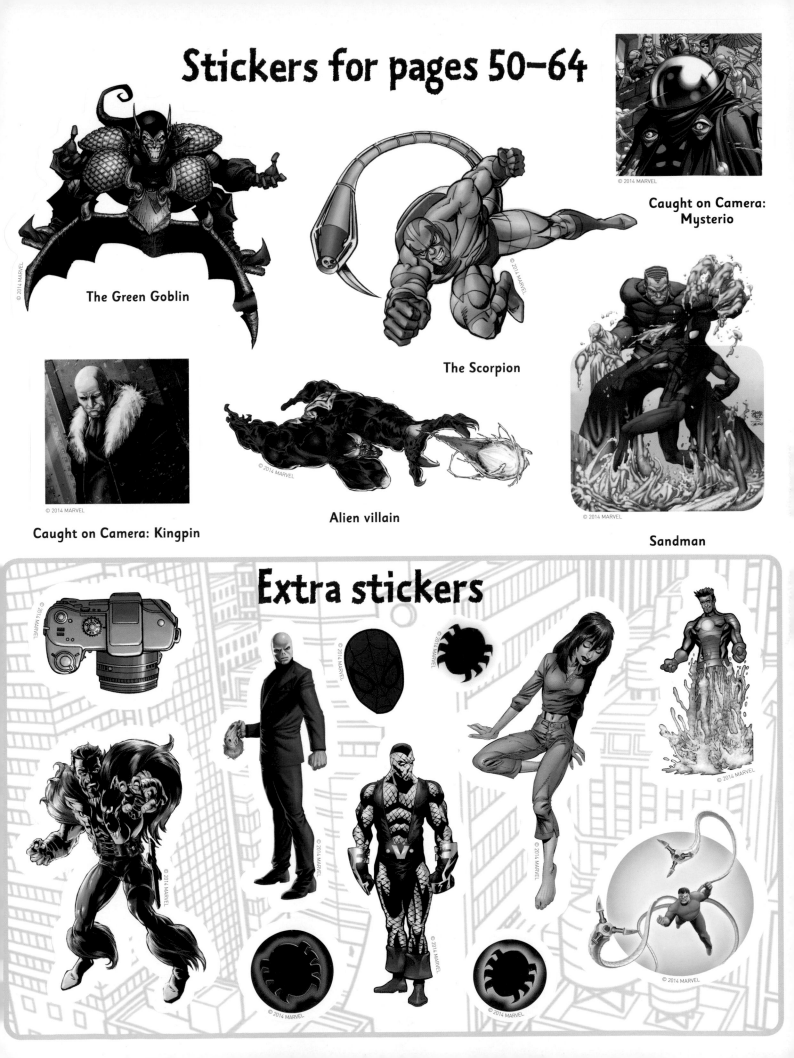

Stickers for pages 50-64

The Green Goblin

The Scorpion

Caught on Camera: Mysterio

Caught on Camera: Kingpin

Alien villain

Sandman

Extra stickers

Extra stickers

Extra stickers